Fields Of Poetry

15 Voices From Across The UAE

Fields of Poetry

Published by Sail Publishing L.L.C.

First published in 2021

Copyright © 2021 by Sail Publishing L.L.C.

All rights reserved. This book or any portion thereof may not
be reproduced or used in any manner whatsoever without the
express written permission of the publisher except for the use of
brief quotations in a book review.

This book uses a font and a layout purposed to make the reading
experience easier for dyslexics, towards an inclusive reading
experience.

ISBN: 978-9948-8692-1-4

UAE National Media Council Permit #: MC-02-01-7908415

Age Classification: +16
The age classification for this book's contents is set in accordance
with the age classification system issued by the UAE's National
Media Council.

Sail
سيل

Email: info@SailPublishing.com
Facebook: facebook.com/SailPublishing
Instagram: @SailPublishing
Twitter: @SailPublishing

Contents

1

Poetry by

Alya Hussain Ali Waheedi

Forget

Try so hard to figure things out
Forget
Get a clear mind

Can't you see it's all in your head
Stand for yourself
Dreams
Dreams of a little girl who was told *don't dare to dream*

You owe her this dream
Or, more so,
Success
Strength
Happiness
Love
Or you may also call it forgiveness

A new start
New adventure
A pursuit to happiness that never ends

That Name

Your name is as nasty as death to a child
And as bad as suffocation
As hard as betrayal
Terrible as your actions

I have been screaming inside my whole life
Weighted by anger and resentment
Swear to never marry any guy who holds your name

Never thought of your name twice
Never wanted to say it out loud
Until I realized running
Hiding
Twirling in pain
Hands on the mouth
Shhh… nobody can hear your pain

Just means living in the past
Bad coping mechanism
Self-abuse and harm

So, I decided to write it on the snow
On a paper
And scream it loud
But the echo answered with a painful voice
He's not the same guy

And continued
You are curing yourself
You are capable of enduring

I Envy Your Brush

I envy your brush
I wish for those hands

I want some colors
And an empty blank surface

I want to swish and swoosh the brush around
Mix this color and that together

Until I see the painting come alive
And my hands so free
Just like it's creating an epic musical sound
Those eyes can speak,
can tell a story
And those clouds so divine
Those flowers so fragile

Can't wait to hold you, my brush
And have an eternity of dancing
An eternity of enchanting the souls and charming the eyes

The Need To Fly

They say you are moving at a fast pace

Don't you get tired
Get some rest
Sleep some more

But oh, if they just knew what I have missed

I want to speed and fly
I want to spread my wings
I want to feel alive
Even if I come over a speed bump, I will keep going

Chase those dreams
Turn them into reality

For sure, the road is rugged and not one line

I might fail and cry, but I will get up
Because real courage is to continue even when it's hard

I don't have time. I need to prove myself to myself
For what has passed of our time is more than what is
remaining

Blessed Misery

To feel
It's my blessing
And my misery

The blessing of misery

I Am A Fool

I was a fool when I thought I could pave my own way into
your heart
I was a fool when I accepted the kind gesture that you
offered

I guess I was so desperate to feel something
Be with someone
Be touched again
But with love and passion
and not be stung with poison
for I have been poisoned enough in my life

Never thought of myself so low
Never bought this bullshit before
Why now you ask

It seems I am all okay, but my self-worth is stuck in the past

I deserve much more than this shallow guy
This unaccomplished job
And these small steps
Just keep on getting smaller and smaller
Just to not outgrow who surround me

Yeah, I am too afraid to fly

I have been so hypnotized my whole life with a false idea

Please others; forget yourself!
But I say please... please
Place yourself first

Stretch that fist
Wave that brush
Keep that smile
And trust God's plan for you

A Cocoon

I have lived an illusion
a misunderstanding for too long

Twisting in pain
Couldn't bear
Focused my energy on blame

The reason is different
Way bigger than I may have thought

It was within me all this time
Directed by feelings & need
Like strings of a wooden toy moving me around

Heart and body are asking me to stop
And mind kept saying we need to keep going

Until I shattered into a million pieces
Couldn't step any further or move anymore

I have taken to my bed, a place to live
A shelter to keep me warm
The perfect haven when life knocks me down

But not too long after hatching out of that cocoon, out of
bed
Found myself again on the streets of life
ready to be fragile
ready to be perfectly imperfect

But Why?

I woke up today feeling excited
Woke up yesterday feeling stressed
And before feeling sad

I have been hunted with different spirits
And infected with mood swings

Can't make up my mind
Heavyweight in the heart
Confusion in the mind

Everyone says I am different except my cat
She finds ways to love me even when I am sad

Am I going crazy?
I can feel a million thing at once
Thinking about how I came up to be
Confused between values and desires
Money and freedom
Me and family

I found a way to remember how I should value myself
above all
Nothing was easy at all
Tiredness
Confusion
And tears but slowly I change

I change like a bee working hard
Giving sweet, sweet honey
But sting when a threat is found

Tomorrow is a mystery
But I wake up by God's will
Doesn't matter happy or sad
The power to open my eyes will lend me more to continue
the day

I woke up today, which used to be tomorrow
Ready to feel
  eady to cry
    ady to try
      dy to change
        y ?

Enlightening

Writing poetry
Reading poetry
Listening to poetry

Is like having a superpower to understand the language of
the hearts
Language of the hurt
Of pain
Of need
Of wisdom
Understanding what's within the line of the lines

Getting to know the beauty of how life has had its ways
with us and had it differently for each of us

But yet we found our ways into each other words and
feelings

Heavy Feeling

Heavy Shoulders
Warm hands
Foggy sight
Foggy mind
And dizzy soul

Yes, I am all of that

They say relax
Preach me it will all pass

It's been three years on the road of healing & desperately
trying to make myself sane again

Tears have become my way of expression
Silence is my way to calm myself down
Sleeping is my haven
And taking an off day is my way of quitting

I found in my family and friends' solace & comfort
A place that I visit when I need to remember who I was,
who I am

Saying to myself you are getting there
You will reach keep moving
Look how far you have come

But strings of the past
Keep pulling me down
Reminding me of what once was
And what could be

Alya Hussain Ali Waheedi is an Emirati poet who has been writing for less than one year. She got inspired by how poetry can be used as a means to deliver feelings and emotions to the listener. She started writing as a way of expressing herself, writing about life experiences and emotions that are usually considered not for sharing.

Poetry by

Balqees Al Bastaki

To Love

I don't know why
when we experience
love's bliss,
we call it "falling".
For to love
is to rise above all.

I don't know why
when we see
love's light,
we call it "blind".
For to love
is to open your eyes
to the only truth.

I don't know why
when we feel
love's embrace,
we call it "captivity".
For to love
is to set your heart free.

I don't know why
when we take
love's path,
we call it "losing ourselves".
For to love
is not to lose yourself,
but to find it in another.

Within

In the journey of life
she let her heart sail away
from the shores of loneliness,
to ride the waves of desire.
She followed desperation
in the wrong direction,
losing herself
to a false destination.
She turned to look back,
but the storm washed away
who she used to be.
She thought she was
once again alone,
only this time,
the sand covered her feet,
the sun kissed her face,
and in the ocean's embrace,
she breathed away her fears.
With no place left to search
but within,
she stopped looking for love,
and started finding it
in herself.
And just when
she started loving herself,
love found her.

An Ordinary Day Of Spring

It was an ordinary
day of spring,
but oh how unordinary
life would become after,
they did not know.
In between the aisles of destiny
they walked,
lost in
trivial thoughts.
Little did they know,
in a fleeting glimpse,
their eyes would lock
and their lives would be
forever changed.
Little did they know,
their souls would recall
a certain moment
a million years ago,
on another plane,
a certain pact they made
to love one another
unconditionally.
Their tongues uttered some words,
but their eyes spoke
a different language,
one of the stars
one of knowing,
of a fairy-tale,
of a love like no other.

Time & Time Again,

Time & time again
I let you win.
Time & time again,
in the face of the unknown
you convinced me
to join your side.
Whenever I stood at a crossroads,
somewhere along my life's path,
you steered me in your direction.
You tried to keep me safe,
but in the shadow of the false safety,
there lived loneliness.
In the shadow of safety
there lived darkness.
Until the day came,
when I had to look you in the eye,
and thank you,
but let you go,
for in the presence of fear,
there can be no home for the
purity of love.

Life Goes On

I remember a time,
when we believed
that pain could kill,
and broken hearts
could never mend.
That life would stop
with every goodbye
and the love in our hearts
would die with a lie.
Yet day after day,
the pain meant healing,
our hearts continued beating,
and the sun kept on shining.
And after every goodbye,
there was a hello.
until we finally understood
the beauty of life,
for despite it all,
it just goes on.

Things

I want to tell you things;
like the number of moments
I think of you
in a day.
The number of times
I want to call,
but hesitate.
The smiles
I try to hide,
but always fail.
I want to tell you things,
but I don't.
I only whisper them
to the wind
and I close my eyes,
knowing
you could still hear me.

To My Father

Little details
and sweet memories
of a time when
you were here,
and the world was
a different place.
Smoky scents,
and your old uniform,
remind me how
everything disappeared
in your embrace.
If I close my eyes,
I can still picture your face,
hear the sound
of your voice,
in every time & space.
If I close my eyes,
I could still feel your love smiling
at us from above
with grace.
If I close my eyes,
I know that deep in my heart
is your place,
just as it was then,
it will forever remain still.

Balqees Al Bastaki is a multi-talented entrepreneur with a passion for the arts. She gave up her 10-year professional career in communications to start her food business as a Pastry Chef. She has a passion for the Culinary Arts, piano playing, painting & poetry.

Poetry by

Hesa Matar Aldahel

Emotional Attachments

It's only when emotions get involved, we stop
Stop evolving
Stop making choices
Stop making sense
Trying to survive
Give up
Lay down
Stay still
Pain ends
And so does the fear of the end

Jigsaw Puzzle

How do I tell them?
It's not you
It's not me
We are a perfect match
Like two pieces in a jigsaw puzzle
That fit together
But don't belong in the same box

Lawn Mowers

They labeled me "grass"
used to fill extra landscapes
and when my head grew taller
filled with dreams, ideas and opinions
they bemoaned it with the rest
breathing in fresh-cut dreams
killers
they mistook my creativity for weeds
they pulled it out
tossed it aside
if they have waited
a small daisy would sprout out
the type of daisy that would make them stop
admire
how something so small
can make you wonder
does creativity come from anywhere?

Missing

When they told me you were gone
I laughed it off
You always come back
But it's been three days
And I'm looking for your tracks

My heart is slowly breaking
Come to me
Whole, unharmed to stop my world from shaking
I am wasting

Find Your Purpose

An important question to ask
What is my purpose in life?
They say "major in this, study that"
"In four years, a job is guaranteed!"
Why was I put on this earth?
I whispered to myself
Was I meant to pray, pray and pray?
And when I have a little spare time
Pray some more
But I need to earn money
Feed myself
Dress my body
Find shelter to dress my sins
To dress me when I don't pray
What is my purpose in life?
Is it to work, work, work?
Have fun then work some more
"don't say I can't, don't say I won't
Be positive
Try, try until you're the best
Try, try until you break
But remember be positive
Be brave"
What's the purpose?

Pages To Fill

You see before you a physical form
Whole
Legs, hips, waist, shoulders
And a swollen head
What you fail to notice
Are the pages hidden in my folds
Waiting to be filled
With the wisdom of the past
The reality of our present
And the disappointments that the future holds

Synesthesia

Black tastes bittersweet
Leaves a memory on my lips
After a kiss
I miss
Black the absence of light
My light
My sight is gone every time I taste black
Melancholic
In my gut
Twisted, bloated, obstruct
By the darkness I swallow
And keep inside
Keeping me hollow
Sore, tired
I bore the black on my skin
Keep it in
Leave me with my sorrow
Expose me not for they've forgot
Picture my head
I will not
Can not
Shall not
See my head at the end of a knot

Hesa Matar Aldahel is an Emirati poet and a member of the "Untitled Chapters" Women writers community. She uses poetry to express her views on mental illness, self-exploration, and her Sphynx cat.

Poetry by

L. Toma

The Privilege Of The Above

It's beautiful to look down from above the fascinating perspective
The lovely details
The gasp - *How small things are*
The realization that you are afraid to go below
They are afraid to fall
And, at the end of the day, do they really care about the *below?*
Do they really want to learn from the *below?*
To discover the hardships, the loss, the pain, the desperation, the isolation?
The black and white of life, of living on the brink of survival
Where you forcefully apply colorful cellophane to bring a new perspective,
Some splotch of normal, even though the colors are off and there is no connection to reality?
You try to tap into the deep knowledge, to build from scratches and remnants,
But the crumbling buildings pile on you
You look above for some hope and help,
But from above, you are just a dot,
If you are even seen at all...
And who wants to practice empathy for a dot?
Who would fall to the below to see you, to hear you?
The bell rang – a loud sound announcing danger, the bearer of deathly news.
Run and hide, and save yourself and take any bits of your heritage with you.
The bell still swings silently, although on the ground, you can still hear the sounds of the hinges.
From above, silence dominates.

They are scared of silence.
They can always edit it.
From above, they can add your sorrowful music to
artificially create a digestible emotion.
Below, the hearts cannot handle emotion anymore.
In this rehearsal of life towards a show that will not happen
You try in vain to reverse the tragedy,
To re-build, to re-live, to try to thrive.
Layers upon layers of rubble do not lead to anything.
Except, maybe, to a fine view from above.

Inspired by Hiwa K: Do You Remember What You Are Burning?
Exhibition hosted at Jameel Arts Centre, in 2021.

Torn

Feeling torn
Between the place where the physical presence exists
And the realm where the heart resides.
Melancholy for a place I've never been to devours my
existence.
My heart has been broken and mended many times,
But the crestfallen line that splits it through is digging deep
into its core.
I read that humans' ultimate need is to belong and all I
know
It is not here I am fully myself.
I've been told it's not about the destination, but about the
journey.
How long must I wander in doubt, uncertainty and a sense
of un-wholeness
Until I can rest for a bit and say
I have arrived.
The destination is elusive and at times, it is slipping through
my fingers
Like the sand in the warm sea water, I am told I must enjoy.
The sun is making a wonderfully colorful spectacle of its
retreat at the margin of the sea and I do my best to take it
all in,
While still thinking of the place where I belong, which I miss
without having ever visited it.
I close my eyes and I know when I finally reach my
destination, I will look back on this moment, and place,
With a sense of longing and feeling undeniably torn.

The Only Word

I have been gifted with a name and armed with knowledge
But my worth is solely defined by the way I enthusiastically
use the only word it seems is allowed for my sisters and I –
Yes.
Any other answer would scare you.
Saying *No* with a full heart, with a voice stripped of
quivering and deprived of explanations
Would be terrifying, as the start of any revolution always is.
Your fear becomes my responsibility,
As a woman, how can I not be nurturing and
understanding?
My *Yes* is never met by yours.
Yes, said the bride, although no one acknowledged the
reluctance in her heart which trickled through her tears.
Yes, said the daughter, and no one heard her internal music.
Yes, said the mother, even though her wisdom extended
beyond this word.
Yes, said the woman who grabbed a seat at the table, and
that is all she could say. Those controlling the remote will
not relinquish their control, so we are unmuting ourselves.
There's power within and we are translating it into words
for those who cannot understand.
The world where someone's privilege should be everyone's
right is not truly alive. The moment will come when the
only word is a choice and not an edict.

Cloudy Weather

When you meditate, the calm, whispery voice invites you
to imagine your mind as the blue sky, and your thoughts as
the clouds
Passing by, moving on, with the backdrop of the celestial
ceiling.
The breathing should move them along.
But my clouds are stubborn.
They are here to stay.
There's no wind of change to make them disappear.
My clouds lack the sense of humor, and do not take the
form of a rabbit,
They are not sweet and there is no cotton candy quality to
them.
They gather together and turn into darkness,
Forcing me to knit light from love, laughter and happy
memories.
My clouds turn heavy and grey and form thunderstorms.
The heavy raindrops fall and flood my heart with dread and
uncertainty,
Sinking hope and positivity into a bottomless pit.
Sometimes, they lead to tornadoes,
Whisking me away and all I find myself waiting for is to feel
the earth under my feet. Even when there are no clouds,
the sky is still hidden behind a haze of pollution or the
thickness of a blanket of fog.
The weather forecast is rarely correct.
It has a mind and a life of its own.
When the blue sky appears,
Its shade the same one that blesses my grandfather's eyes,
It is so deep, I allow myself to drown,
To let it invade my lungs, my heart, my mind,

Until it reaches my hand and extends it to create an
umbrella
Out of gratitude, and self-love
To shield me from the upcoming cloudy weather.

The Extension

If only we could unplug the dream once we are awakened,
To stop it from haunting us into the day.
How can a manifestation of the darkness not be afraid of
the light?
This unruly child crosses beyond the realm it belongs to.
The most immaterial of things, made from the material of
reality, capture such vivid textures
Through the unimaginable sounds, the unforgettable
words, the images which cannot be unseen,
Echoing loudly in the empty space they come to dominate.
Reality reaches its full circle
Life experiences hauntingly shape our dreams,
Which in turn extend their tentacles over the matrix we
reside in.
The more we live, the more we dream
The more we dream, the more we extend ourselves to
become real.

L. Toma *is a global citizen, passionate about learning, education, and writing. Her personal journey is a collection of moments gathered through living in three countries and traveling in over 30. She is currently based in Dubai, United Arab Emirates, running her own consultancy in learning experience design. She is the master of Cosmos – a lovable, smart, and stubborn Arabian Mau.*

Poetry by

Noura AlMulla

Off

You drifted away
We lost the connection
I tried to switch the lights back on
But you cut the cords
Hid them away
It drove me insane
I stayed in the dark for so long
Looking for the cords that you took away
To switch the lights back on
But I could not
No matter how hard I tried to look
It was pitch black
And I continued to search
I bruised myself
I cut myself
Because I could not see
Then I decided to sit still
To wait for you
Hoping that you would come back
And switch the lights back on
But I waited
And waited
To no response
To no avail
And I was sitting still
Thinking of when the lights switched off
Thinking if I did anything wrong
Blamed myself for it all
Screamed my soul out
Cried a stream
Was it a nightmare?

Was it a dream?
But you never came
So I stopped looking
I stopped waiting
Wishing it was a nightmare
Wishing it was a dream.

Why Don't You Speak?

They pluck your feathers
One by one
And ask
"Why aren't you able to fly?"
They throw their burdens at you
And ask
"Why aren't you able to breathe?"
They quench you
And criticize your darkness
They eclipsed you
And complain about your dimness
They depart you
And ask
"Where have you been?"
They silence you
They silence you
They silence you
And ask
"Why don't you speak?"

A Love That Is Lavender

A kiss on the hand
A kiss on the head
Prayers sent to the skies
Wearing all red
Lavender aroma
Silver and white strings
Food for the soul
Warmth and love
Weightless breath
Never a burden
Good night
Bless you
I miss you.

On Grief

Everyone tells you that grieving takes time
They tell you that time heals all
But they don't tell you how to cope with grieving nor loss
They don't tell you that you suddenly get triggered and
waves of immense sadness and emotions take over you
They don't tell you that you will end up mourning during a
meeting
They don't tell you that most details in your everyday life
will remind you of them
They don't tell you that you will always be in denial about
their passing
They don't tell you that you will keep checking up on them,
only to find out that they are actually gone
They don't tell you that the ache will suffocate you
physically
They don't tell you that you will lose the true essence of life
They don't tell you that you'll fall
You'll lose
You'll mourn
You'll grieve
You'll die.

Thee

Thee, with thy wrecked soul
With the wounded heart as though stabbed with a dagger
Thee, with the intentions as pure as gold
With the hands that have held tremendous pain and will
continue to hold on
Thee, with those eyes
O, thy brown eyes weep nothing but despair
Thee, with those gentle words
That makes the sun rise within the disturbed
Thee, that spends all the sleepless nights
Thinking of thy past, present and the future
Thee, with their falls
Thee, with their honesty
Thee, with their legacy.

Dying Soul

My soul feels tired
The sea within me is drying up
My thoughts are devouring every inch of me
There are no more twinkles in my eyes
My ambitions are fading
My dreams are breaking
And what are hopes anyway?
I have no place or person to call home
My heart is burned out
I no longer speak to the sea
Salt no longer runs through my veins
The flowers in my lungs are resting in peace
I am returning to dust
I am returning to the stars.

Et Tu, Brute?

Breathe in
Breathe out
I tell myself
Breathe in
I try to process all the lies I've been told
Breathe out
I remember all the words you said
My breaths are becoming shorter
My heart is pumping faster
Blood gushes through my head
Your hopes strangle me
Leaving me breathless
I cannot think
I cannot speak
I do not breathe
Et tu, Brute?
I end

My Safe Haven

My safe haven was never a place
It was never a house
It was never a thing
My safe haven has flesh
It has bones
My safe haven has veins and blood running through them
My safe haven has a particular smell
Perfumed with musk and oud
My safe haven has the most beautiful eyes
Brown and spiraled with specks of golden sunlight
My safe haven was never a place
It is not a house
My safe haven is you.

Aching For You

I ache for your sweet presence
I ache for the feelings you make me feel and the stories you
tell
I ache for the stars above your head and the sand beneath
your feet
I ache for your laughter
For your smile
I ache for your twinkling eyes
For your golden heart
For the love you held and the love you gave
I ache for your touch
For your wisdom
I ache for your sweet memory.
– 11/2001

Spring Again

I feel my walls slowly breaking
Leaking the water of the roaring sea within me
Rays of the sun start peeking through
The trees inside of me are blooming
My clouds are not grey anymore
The snow is melting
My waterfalls are flowing
The fire is put out
The rose never perished
It's spring again.

Noura AlMulla is a fond admirer of written words. Her writings usually flow through when she meets the sea. Noura's writing journey began as a child through her love for reading. In 2015 she created her own blog where she mostly publishes relatable poems that tackle loss, grief, and love.

Poetry by

Omar Albeshr

Curve Of Light

To stare sheer beauty in the eye,
Your perfect smile shines so bright.
I feel in awe, so much that I,
Will never forget your beautiful sight.

I peek through your soul,
When your eyes take me in.
I feel lost and lose control,
When your ray starts to fill me in.

Reborn in that sweet moment,
Revived by your heavenly beam.
Wrapped between the joy and torment,
If your heart, like mine, would only gleam.

Your brown fringe tickles your face,
As it waves and dances with the wind.
Oh, what lucky curls for they
Have felt her grace.

And that magical smile that dazzles the sky,
Made the moon and stars want to hide.
But they'd peek and pry; in the distance, they'd spy,
To find why your smile is so profound.

And the night lingers on and on,
Because the sun is shy to rise.
Unable to match your beautiful dawn,
She asks the clouds to be her guise.

Rotten Shame

My heart grows colder and colder,
My nightmares are getting bolder.
All the desolation of creation rests on my shoulders,
I writhed alone, but I wish I had told her.

That demons slithered within me,
And took nest in my chest.
I cower and hide, not wanting them to see,
How I wear this rotten shame like a crest.

Untold Fairy Tale

A fairy tale untold,
A love story that was never meant to unfold.
A child that breathed his last too soon,
A day that never made it to noon.

My Moon And I

My moon and I, we're in tune,
Fills my sky, brushes my dune.
My moon balances my moods and my tides,
When my moon appears, and when my moon hides.

Always around me, and within,
Even when my moon is cloaked, or thin.
But when my moon comes out in full sight,
In an ample form, there is no match for my delight.

Her Slave

I fell in love with the woman inside this girl,
Then I fell even harder for the girl inside this woman.
I had to look; to remove the shells to see the pearls,
To search inside and find the riches deeply hidden.
And I gaze upon her, as mortals behold the moon,
When she bestrides the dawdling nomadic clouds.
To glimpse the stark image of her that is immune,
To time, age, or whatever life might wage upon us helpless
crowds.

She looks at me with those radiant eyes, and I am her slave,
What sweeter prison would hold me as her featherlike
embrace?

Within these arms lies my home which my heart eternally
craves,
Such untouchable moments inhibit me, and with my soul,
they interlace.
In love, I was, even before my thoughtless senses
celebrated it.
In love, my heart rejoiced, and in love, my being was
illuminated.
Identifying it made me stronger, it made me gain passion
and grit.
Nothing could derive my love, surely not this love,
impeccably fated.

Laced With Tears

In my own dim world,
I lie still,
In silence,
Only my heartbeats,
Echoing in my ears.
Overflowing thoughts,
Whirling,
As they spill,
Within my iris,
Grinding defeats,
Laced with tears.

Bashful Lover

You sit close to me
Yet
Your bashful eyes never
Fully return my gaze.
You yearn to look
But
Your brave heart suffers
Love in its early days.
Our hearts, since we've met
Changed in rhythm
and forever
Would fill our lives in mysterious ways.

Prognosis

This is the life that you presaged,
The pain and anguish you had signified.
But I thought it was just an imprudent forecast,
But it was true, and I was diminished with a blast.

Clueless as to how you achieve,
To know beforehand, the aching grief.
How you predict each tormenting throb,
So painful that I feel my heart will stop.

Have I been cursed by your evil eye?
That changed the mirth into a cry.
You stole my marrow, and left me petrified,
You added sorrow and left me mystified.

Have you bewitched me to lose my helm?
And be the ill-fated hero in this tragic film.
So that I live like the dead but at the utmost fear,
That you'll say the word, and death would be near.

Nomads

The sun guides the nomads,
And at night the stars take their hands.

With courage and poetry in their hearts,
They lived and died by the swords and verse.
A line could make them dine with kings,
A line could strike them with a curse.

Atop the golden dunes,
Across the foreign lands.
Traveled for many moons,
Dodging goons and quicksands.

I touch her land and speak to the wind,
What of her, and where she went.
I look for what's left behind,
And I follow her scent.

Nothing would hinder me or slow me down,
Not the rainfall with its silver darts.
Not the beasts that are roaming around,
I will trounce them all and pierce their hearts.

Until I reach your tribe's canvas tents,
An eerie feeling overcomes me, a chill runs through my
bones.
As I hear them speak of you in the past tense,
And point towards a grave marker made of stones.

Nothing is the same, nothing feels right,
Nothing is worth for my heart to pound.

I collapse by the gravesite,
My tears wet the ground.

The sun ceases to guide this nomad,
Even the stars at night gave up taking his hand,
Because there is nothing that can be done,
To mend the heart of this broken man.

Dreams Of Spring

The winds of winter,
blew away,
the hopeful dreams of spring.

A breath, a whisper,
of a new day,
Yet no bird dares to sing.

These feelings linger,
Clocks astray,
Pendulums never swing.

I point my finger,
That's the way,
I can hear a faint ting.

Let's cross this river,
Then we may,
Revive old dreams of spring.

Omar Albeshr *is an Emirati from Abu Dhabi, he holds a degree in Avionics Engineering, currently works in Tourism. Writing has always been a passion for him since he was really young. He has recently published his first poetry book titled "Taintlessness".*

Poetry by

Ammarah Safa

Till I Rise

Till I rise
I shall fall continuously,
Not efficiently nor forgivingly,

With the presence of silence
and the agony of peace
found at the stroke of midnight
setting me free.

Be it a month or few
the hope will linger in me
with all my fears,
with all the tears,

I will rise
only to be grounded by heart
In love and priorities

It is in you as it is in me,
getting closer and stronger
Open ye eyes,
to seek the truth
Let's all work to not be uncouth.

Ubiquitous

The golden blaze that hits me every time i pray,
seeks me onto His way

As i kneel by dawn with an open heart for His remembrance
I find myself meditating in semblance

A reflection of His love i find in winds that sway past me,
helping me breathe out the toxin in me

I admit to not have seen Him
but surely He has always been
Through my toughest fights
Through the longest nights

In a world that believes in happily ever after
I am rooting for the Hereafter
All the duas and deeds
All the nights spent in solemnity longing to be the one
under His shade
On the day when everything shall fade.

Salvation

I got killed for devotion
and was healed with the same reason
my high is the highest I have ever been,
and my low is the lowest I can ever go,
Just like the way waves flow
I thought you would know,
in the way I glow.

A brush of glitter,
A slide of shimmer
above all the balderdash and the chaos,
there for me as for you,
to believe in one another is what we need to do.

I have been falling,
but falling isn't failing
It is learning and unearthing,
How many times have we failed to realize the echo of life?
That life is no coincidence,
but an outcome of our choices.

So Long, Hope

i am not who you think i am
i have layers that go deeper than the surface of the earth
i have stories that run into my roots
i have memories that restore my hope but uproot my life

hope,
the single most dangerous feeling ever learned
it dreads me throughout my bad days
it slowly poisons me for it is not what it seems to be

hope is not happiness
hope is not peace
hope is love,
it is the breeze

but hope, you come in different colors and shapes
someday you are the prince standing outside my blue
castle
yet on others you are the demon
hiding behind my back
creeping on me, waiting for the night to fall

mostly you are me
and i am you
you leave trails in my mind like treasures to find
why should i find you?
why should i hope for better days?

i will no longer be you,
i will not hope,
for the dreams my heart desires

for the moments i long for
as they all eventually crumble down meeting the harsh
reality of this world.

Abandoned

Mystical layers of secrets
holy drops of courage
all around mixed with the breeze
peaceful as it may be
with its own sticks and stones on the loose
rocking us all
towards the shore

reflection of the sea in all the maybes
the moon shining in the shade of yellow
beyond the light mellow
the sticks and stones all lead to the visibility
buzzing of the bees gives it serenity

from here, the roads seem to lead nowhere
the peace seems to get established in the very same breeze
as i reach closer to where i am supposed to be
my heart is left behind to weave,
for the fabric of my being
is beyond the seen.

Let Go

confined in the walls i see,
a million dreams and breaths taken by thee,
with every year that passes by,
the reflection of bygone memories fades along
and we grow,
we understand and be understood,
we learn and we let go,
i may have touched undignified lives,
i may have burnt a thousand times,
surely the remorse doesn't show.

yet how do i let go?
do i forget?
do i forgive?
or do i accept?
some accusations and some beliefs,
but none tell me what to leave,
with sorrowful eyes and white lies,
these series of questions never fail to bring me on my
knees,
despite all that i believe.

Twelve

white and clear,
the perfect color
a blink of someone I fear
still standing tall and clear,

It is daunting the way I felt underwater
an emotion I never bother,
It came as a dragon to pull me into its dungeon,
but little did I know its intention

merely it was to hurt me,
rather it meant to scare me,

with the noise
with the void
and with the choice

I reminisce how pure white was
before it showed me its true color
the form I will never forget,
nor the one I want to remember.

Wings

As I stand on the podium of life,
blaring questions and blazing battles I see
running along the maze of my mind,
just like leaves that are entwined

It is here to clip off my wings
if only I could feel something
I would be heard,
I could be loved,
if only I felt the thing

but I know my life is designed,
the way spiraling snowflakes are defined.

Therefore, here I lay, speaking from the depths of despair,
where there is nothing found to repair.

Portrait

My body is the canvas of my life
from birthmarks to scars,
some display the beauty of the early years,
others remind me of the battles that i could endure.

This canvas is not a beautiful one,
rather it is the ostentatious one.

Be that as it may,
for i shall not crash my guard down in any way,
nonetheless, i understand that one needs to be strong
enough on the inside to love someone on the outside.

Through

moonlight shone on my face
with the distance carefully placed
through the dreams in my eyes that I chase,

the clutches still reckon with me,
for it will ever be,

at times I am walking through a haze,
unable to realize it is a maze,

a game played by the weak and lonely,
searching for something a little more homely
yet I learned not so long ago,
the art of not letting go.

Ammarah Safa *is a young adult who has a writing experience of 3 years. She hopes to take up writing full time.*

Poetry by

Harshini Akshinthala

In Another Life

Is this madness I sense?
A passion for more
A hope forever after
Creating desires, I can't cater to.
This amenable calling
Born from your beguiled charisma
Descends upon me, ensnaring
Like a mouse in the fox's snare.
Was it fortitude or destiny?
Seems frivolous for what follows
As I hold my sword
Against your beating heart.
For my loyalties lay afar
While yours lie to the rival entity
A conflict of interest has left me lovelorn
Left me torn and drained
So inopportune yet so serenely preordained.
How do I begin to explain?
How much love can this poor heart bear
For we meet in another life
Where odds are in our favor
Clemency comes at a price
A price as heavy as one can imagine.
I turn the poisoned blade towards me
Getting one final look at your face
Accepting this crooked fate for all I sinned
I devour the blade
While this poison of the unrequited
Seeps into my veins
And to wake up in another life.
Only this time, with you.

The Trodden Horse Of Thy Betrothed

The butterflies spring to life
The world lightens up
The stars shine a little brighter
Is it just me or did the moon just smile?
Smiling to say I have seen the enamored, for a thousand
years
Some stayed true for as long as I shined
Some faded before my next nightfall
All started with the promise of eternity and after
I stare astounded, finding it hard to believe
But no time did I have
I run down the hill on the cool grass
I feel the dew tickling my skin
My hair flies disheveled, indifferent to the words of the
Lunar Queen
I approach the shore where I see the vast sea
I hear the trodden horse of my betrothed
I quiver to the evening chill
But there's a warmth beneath this drowsy love
How I could melt from this warmth
Like a candle left alone to illuminate the world
I look him in the eye, everything feels right
His beautiful chiseled face and the impeccable smile
Ever so joyful ever so full of life
He gets down from the horse and embraces
And just like that, a strong gale shook me into senses
I saw myself standing all alone
I felt the air weigh heavy with affectation
No sign of Elijah or the horse
Just the daze of the infinite stars and Lunar Queen
Looking down on me with pity.

The Smell Of Rain

The smell of rain reminds me of home,
The indecipherable feeling of comfort

Petrichor, the earthly scent
Brings me to rest
"Things change, people change"
The good old saying remains unclear
When young, naïve and trust all that appears
Living my normal life, fighting my battles and attempting to
adapt
New relations too fragile while the old ones fade into dust

Discovering the comfort I've been yearning for
Is found in this insignificant endeavor
Which I exploit to feel better

The one thing that is constant is the smell of rain

Makes me reminisce about all I have

Grandparents so loving and forgiving,
Always got my back,
Oversee that my parents cut me some slack

Aunts and Uncles, spoiling me with all I wanted and would
ever want
Caring and adoring me like their own

Brothers and Sisters been with me through thick and thin
Lift the weight of stories from my back

Recollect the same memories again and again
Knowing their worth is worth our time

My parents, the incarnations of the divine
Love so unconditional, Love so pure

I smell the Petrichor
I see the grey splotches of cloud
The green trees complementing the color
I feel the first drops on my skin,
The cool breeze dancing gracefully against my face
I hear thunder and it only gets loud
As if telling me to move on, the show is over

Through the journey of life, we travel by the road of
uncertainties
Our choices may end in doom or bloom
But make sure to hang on right
To the ones you love and believe in
Before the storm of age hit

Wandering Mind

The hot sun blazing on my face sets me to ease with you
Knowing you'll be beside me, made my feelings recede

We were dancing under the moonlight
Wishing the sun would never rise
But you had to leave.
The sun came up and went back down
But this time I was all alone under the moonshine

I await you under the beam of the moon
Knowing deep inside you would, but alas I am wrong

My mind wanders in the fields of endearment we harvested
together

The cool breeze filled with our memories,
Gently touches the warmth of my skin
Only to stab me hard again
Although ephemeral if I have a chance, I would live through
it over again.

Where Are You Now?
[In the loving memory of my beloved grandfather]

"You were the light in my darkest times
Abandoned your pleasures for me
A proud moment of truth
When your values run in my veins
Advice in abundance, lavish amount of appreciation
Both of which define your heart
Your excellent trait of discipline
Wish I'd inherited it.
You banished the wind, so I don't flicker
But where are you now,
When I'm roaring might?
I am indeed blessed, by the heavens above
To be guided by a mentor like you.
I shall forever be grateful for the shelter under your
patronage
For I carry the hope with me evermore
As I long to see you again someday
You will always hold a place in my heart
No one else will ever fill
Always remember, I will love you forever and after"

Sea Of Uncertainty

Drowning in the sea of uncertainty
Forgetting that I can swim
Confusion filling every inch of me
With the sudden shock paralyzing me
Now it is too late to do anything
Too cold for surviving
Black clouds of misery
Look down on me in victory
In a distance, I see a boat approaching
In the boat I see a man with a rope.
The beacon of hope;
I cried out and knew this was the chance
The man managed a glance and rowed back disappearing
in the distant fog
The cold water numbing my senses
I felt my blood clogging
I felt the grief ripping my soul into bits languorously
Well then I felt nothing
I sank into the abyss of the sea where no one would find me
Because my absence went unseen

Harshini Akshinthala is an aspiring author, born in 2004, who hails from Hyderabad, India, and was brought up in Dubai. She is an avid reader who relishes writing and dreams of publishing her own book one day. She has a lust for life and is interested in learning new languages, exploring new places, and loves immersing herself in beautiful diverse cultures. She is also passionate about Space and the cosmos; it enchants and fascinates her about the wonders and possibilities that lie in the infinite great beyond.

Poetry by

Roudha AlMarzouqi

Trophies

Why is our society so obsessed with trophies?
Win in competitions and matches just to get prizes
They say: "It's a gift, a surprise!"
But they are all lies
Why do we feel proud when we get a medal?
It should not make us feel proud,
it is just a piece of metal
Why do we celebrate when we get awarded?
But we do not celebrate our daily accomplishments
Why wait for a trophy
To give you a sense of joy and fulfillment?
I am guilty of feeling that way too
Win a trophy, one or two
Feel the self-validation
For a moment or two
And yearn for a bigger title
to feel a boost of confidence
It is a good feeling,
to be celebrated by other people
But they are not going to make you gleeful
For your whole life
So you have to learn the art
Of celebrating each step and start
As time went on
I realized that the best prizes
Are the ones that are small
The happiness in your parents' eyes
The laughs and smiles
Of the people you love
These are the most worthwhile
These are the accomplishments

That should be celebrated too
They matter the most
Because they almost happen daily
But we fail to realize them
Because we grew up feeling a sense of self-validation
Only when we win a competition across a nation
Those competitions and races teach you
That you should celebrate the things you learn too
You should be proud of yourself
and celebrate every step, and every obstacle you overcome
Because the small steps make the biggest ones matter the
most
They are the ones that caused the biggest waves
Because in the beginning, they started as small ripples.

Little Bird

There is a bird in me that yearns to fly high
And wave to the real-world a good-bye

It flies through the meadows and mountains
Through rivers and oceans

It flies over dauntless, brave soldiers
Fighting shoulder to shoulder

It reminds this little bird of bold boulders
This bird discovers new surroundings
And fights in countless battles
With its heart pounding

You might be wondering,
How did this little bird fight?
While it was made only for flights

Well, this little bird was in its nest
While laying its head to rest.
It traveled through the world,
And experienced the underworld

Because it held a book
And that was all it took.

Void Of Darkness

There is a sun inside each of us
That shines the brightest in our happiest days
But is replaced by the moon
in our darkest

Yet, some people do not have a sun
But instead, a void so deep with darkness
That the moon cannot be found

They try to fill their empty, dark voids
By dimming other people's suns
Till their suns are not replaced by a moon
Instead by a darkness soon to be like theirs

They project their darkness
Towards other people
Until they fill them with sadness

What those people don't realize
Is that other people's suns
Do not take away from their own

All Colors

I love all colors.
In all shades and ranges.
I love the color orange
when the sun rises
and spreads its orange rays across the sky.

When in the early morning,
the orange tree waves to me
as the wind blows against its oranges
decorating its skirt of leaves
and popping out between the leaves
like pearls on a dress
to impress

I love the color blue,
as deep as the ocean,
as blue as someone's ocean eyes.
Deceptive at times,
blue, a color so mysterious,
deep and dark
pulls you in without a remark

I love the color pink,
I find it on my friend's cheeks as she blushes.
As the blood rushes to her face as we speak
I find it in the cherry blossoms of the fields
in my dreams

I love the color yellow,
as bright as the sunshine on a summer evening,

as bright as the stretch of the smile on my friend's face,
reaching her twinkling eyes
but not as rich as my friend's golden heart

I love the color red,
as deep and rich as the rubies,
as dark as the roses we see in movies
I stare at the fierceness
and boldness of the red dresses
that receive astounded expressions

I love the color green,
the color of life and gleam.
The color of plants and trees.
I love the green that decorates everything
that brings life to earth and everything in between
Green is life itself
It is the color of ecosystems,
habitats and the base of all biosystems

But under all that green, is brown
A color looked down upon,
yet it holds the richest of the world's gold,
not the red rubies or the blue sapphires,
but it is the base of all the green that brings life to us.

You see, colors work hand in hand
to bring beauty to the lands
I cannot choose one color
Because all colors have characteristics of their own

They carry themselves differently,
yet so brilliantly each one is.
Each color holds memories,
each one decorates our reveries
But you cannot picture a scene in life
with one color only
more often than not,
you will see another color popping out.

Women

Women,
what word do I use to describe?
A whole gender,
that was classified
And said to belong in certain places
A woman is an entity of success
Not a person wearing a dress
Or being "girly" to impress
A woman is the epitome of braveness
Ask of a mother protectiveness
Her resilience and persistence
Ask of a girl that fought to be heard
In a world where she was taught that her voice is
insignificant
Despite all the odds,
she grew up to be magnificent
So do not tell me a woman belongs in a place
Because she was not born to replace
Each woman is different
But there is something they all share
They all have a heart, of warriors

The Moon And The Sun

The moon called out to the sun
As the time for dawn ensued
But the sun was too hesitant
To show itself again in its element
After a night of the moon
That has gone by too soon

You see,
the moon was loved by all
Divine, delicate, and exquisite
Silver-white in the starkness of the night
Illuminating the path of everything in sight

The sun compared itself to the moon
And failed to see the day of gloom
When it hid behind the clouds
Too shy, to be seen between the crowds

The sun is not just a light
Its lightness itself, so bright
It is the light after the dark
Igniting all sparks of hope
hope for another day
another chance for a gateway

But it failed to see its beauty
In all its brightness and glamour
Because it compared itself
To something incomparable
The moon has its own charm
But so does the sun

But it failed to see itself in its full form
Its ability to transform
The abandonment of the soul

Sunrise is a chance for another day
A hope in display
So, when the sun rose for another day
And shone in its full glory

The blossoms flourished in fields of greens
Kids swam in the warm streams
People accomplished their long-sought dreams
All under the daylight's warm beams

Thus, after a day of glee
The sun called on to the moon
As the darkness loomed on

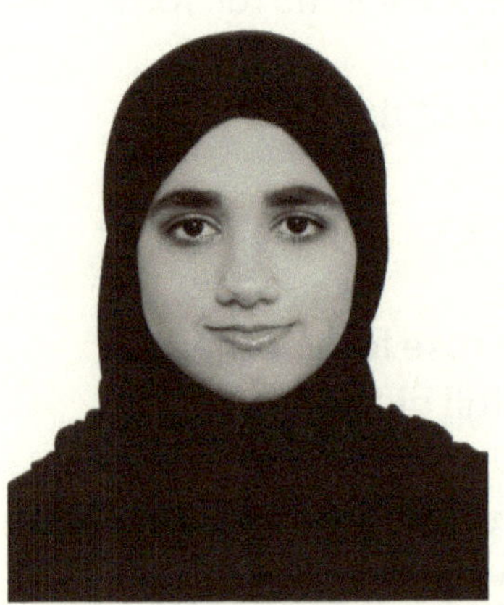

Roudha Almarzouqi has a passion for writing poetry that grew over the years. She uses poetry as a medium to express herself and to raise awareness about critical issues. Additionally, she has participated in numerous poetry competitions and writing programs across the UAE, one of which is the Fifty's Writers Program by the Ministry of the Education. She believes that poetry is a great gateway for the youth to express their emotions since it has a depth that distinguishes it from other mediums. She hopes to publish her own poetry book in the future to inspire others to pursue their dreams in writing.

Poetry by

Shadha Zawawi

Paper Boats

Remember the time when we embraced the storm
And set to sail in those little ponds of turbulence
Our paper boats
Frail with unguarded hopes and fears
Vulnerable and so weak

We set them to sail
In harsh rivers of reality
That we built with our tiny hands
The touch of all the infirmities of our soul
And Innocence
A construction of love and purity

We set them to sail
To reach unknown destinations
Untapped boundaries
How naïve! How sublime!
To sail to the deep ends
On delicate foundations
Thin and disintegrating

We engineer our hearts
With hard enduring material
Defeats and hopes entwine
Strength debilitating
While we still wait at the shores of fate
To see our paper boats
Sail through the test of time

Spring

I am the lone tree
Caught between the crossfire
Of fall vs winter
Refusing to give in
To your coldness
Still bursting with color
In the hope
Of Spring

The Sunset

They say truth and lies
Are like black over white
Each distinguishable
Like day from night
But have you been watching the sunset lately?
When the sun surrenders to the moon
To take charge
When the sky is neither all blue
Or all dark
It is merging with colors of pink, yellow, purple, red
In different intensities
Different shades
Each day
The same sky
But no horizon is the same -
The unsteadfast
My friend if you ask what color is truth
The answer is not black and white
And I would recommend you to instead
Watch the sunset.

Shadha Zawawi, who grew up in the UAE, was introduced to Urdu poems by her mother who used to read to her couplets of great poets such as Mirza Ghalib and Allama Iqbal. As an advocate and law professional, she switches from legalese to poetry in her spare time. While she writes poems in English, to this day Urdu poetry serves as her primary source of inspiration. She also enjoys reading translated versions of Arabic and Persian prose, which she feels connected to.

Poetry by

Tasnim Shahid

Him

When the world changed, so did we
His love drained when mine flowed in
The door to my soul was wide open
As it dignified when he was by my side
Laughter was all we needed
Sweet kisses, small talk and midnight secrets
The harsh taste of love was an unforeseen risk
but oh! myself was too naïve to feel it
Those wounding words are lucid still
As he mouthed, *I am done with this!*
My mind bounced up and down
Had I just swallowed a suicide pill?
A reservoir of love had been wasted
foolish as he is, not to pardon
Nevertheless, he remains, the reasons for my dry and
coldness
Yet all this I know truly,
will only ever appear as a vague memory of my mind's
obscurity.

The Unforeseen Tragedy

It felt like words were ricocheting in my head, an endless
number of thoughts wanting to come out,
Free themselves into the world and come alive
For people to read the pathetic, wailing cries.
Blurting myself on any surface where my marks would
remain, maybe people will finally pay attention.
But then I became the victim of an incurable curse,
Those words vanished, and nothing can ignite my bulb nor
can words form from the tip of my tongue.
Am I still the same, or have I lost it all?
Frantically search a crowd of people for inspiration, a divine
purpose.
Even a simple lyric could turn things the other way.
Will they start to emerge again? Regardless, like
a flickering candlelight,
my thoughts will just nullify as they disappear into a void
I cannot access.
In the state of being vacuous, I keep forcing an alleged
artistry,
Perhaps I've simply strayed away.
When the heart flutters no more, nothing moves me
anymore.
A chaotic cacophony of beats, not beating to their purpose
though.
A feeling that might engulf me again,
Till then, *Thoughts*, can't you become indelible?
So that I may not lose you to my subconscious, the foggy or
the noxious.

Downpour

calmly pours down my windows
tapping, calling to me
as if signaling me to come out.
all my loneliness drains away,
like soft raindrops.

I leave my room finally
to see the outside world that neglects me;
every day, bored without a friend.
rain washes me, makes me pure
creating new friendship bonds, that I pray don't diminish
away.

trace dried raindrops on my windowpane
like stained tears that often run down my face;
all have the same meaning.
because I know I've become one

with the outside world once again.

The Bluest Eye

In every song she hears, every poem she reads
A girl with blue eyes described so beautifully;
Irises vast and deep like the waving ocean.
A blue-eyed damsel in our fairy tales,
Rare as a gem and treasured by men.
The girl reading this can't help but want them too,
for someone to treasure her plain brown eyes like no one
else ever would.

"How unique I would've seemed, but I'm nothing but me."

She is need of knowing that her dilated pupils
are dimensional
and unknown like a black hole.
A pinch of hazelnuts, or
precious metallic gold found deep underground; they dig
all day to find nothing but—molds
A chocolate flavor that they can't endeavor.
Your eyes still shine with the same intensity.
Although you can find plenty with doe eyes, we don't look
into them to realize,
the hint of sparkle that they ignite.
I wish they'd see its specialty like I do, because

your eyes are more than just colors, a doorway to your soul.

Quiet Luminance

Under stars, flying fairy dust that I dream of,
all emerge from a dark cloud;
Lay out the pieces as they conjoin naturally.
Leaves me bewildered,
Constellations are paths to our fates, fatality.

Love ignites a shimmering light,
The stars share my destiny
I count them like sheep till I sleep;
the ordained feeling of loneliness
Resides in me.

Breathe rhythmically or float meticulously
the Moon is a crescent under my gloomy gaze;
The skies are never lonely, because
every little creation is part of a bigger picture.

The bright lanterns in the mesmerizing night
reflect a glisten of euphoria inside my eyes
So that I can bring myself to smile, and stare at little fairy dust
Through this maze, I can foresee unspeakable things,
As I lay under the quiet skies and stars tonight.

From: The Moon, To: You

When did the Earth and the Moon become such good friends?

We're always seen together, in the microcosmos of our
friendship that lays out the stories of our hardships.

I will forever be the Moon to give you light and despite my
shadows & wounds that are revealed in the night, I stay
strong to give you what you deserve.

Revolving around you every second, minute, hour
to eternity; a natural pull in the universe makes
me gravitate towards your direction.

And the cloudy skies surely covers me sometimes,
But shall you wait another night or continue on without
me, it'll be your choice.

The Earth is beautiful with its blossoming flowers and clear
blue skies
while I live with a gloomy aura, as the black sea roars with
all its might.

The blanket of darkness covers me, concealing my inner
depths;
and unlike you, they always fail to explore me.

I know now,
You were made to understand my past and live
the future with me;
Fated in the stars is our story that I'll rewrite over thousands
of pages if I must.

But you will never see my light fade out, or even if I were
to vanish my dearest friend,
know that you can see me in the constellations and wish on
a star for my unforgettable presence.

The Rising Poplar

At the start of time, I sprouted free
breaking through soil, rising with glee.

Branches stretched, like my imaginations
of being full and wild like carnations.

The whistling wind played with my hair, as the turf tickled
my feet
playful children sprinted around, leaning on me for shade
from the heat.

My hair curled upwards, fluttering to the sky
In this solemn forest, I became a social butterfly.

As I met fall, my branches were bare
like trees that stood, in despair.

In mornings I awoke, and horizons were clear
I began to feel empty, as my friends disappeared.

The brown grass stung my eyes, as my reminiscence floated
through my mind,
my roots grasped the dirt.

Shiny black shoes moved swiftly
birds' tweets perished along with me.

*Why did I think they liked me, when this is all they ever wanted
from me*
Now, the truth is all I see.

But don't worry, this is not a farewell,
My charming spirit will return yet again.

A Remedy That Awaits

Autumn is around the corner, and leaves are finally falling in
a graceful manner.
With some hot drinks and a pinch of cinnamon in all my
treats,
As the condensation on the window fades slowly.
I can finally let you go, and
wipe my slate clean.

I remember when you last held my hand,
as our boots scrunched the dead leaves.
Every season leaves its charm behind, but your absence
leaves nothing but a lack of sincerity.

You may have thrown my leaf away and betrayed my trust,
but I'll collect all of them in my backyard and ensure they
make a remarkable scenery.
I'll turn your not-so-pretty work into art,
With poetry and words that'll make you apologize as you
knock on my door for a new start.

Deceitful Love

He is unsure of what to expect,
if her eye smile is simply a sketch or
if her bright red lips are too hard to resist.
Can they love without a doubt;
and through doors he crosses many limits to free her from
her insecurities,
Her heart remains concealed, but her smile is
just solemnity.
He will be aboard the journey with her,
she ever so secretly wishes to not go;
Again by using her little gestures,
His heart will flutter again like the thin pages of her secret
diary,
The truth untold, will perhaps finally unfold.
His tight grip and integrity will be overseen, as she
Continues to fight her internal conflict; controlled by
a blind love,
He fails to keep himself composed as his heart slowly yet
painfully shatters to the floor.
Her eyes glaze over, an icy feeling that pierces him.
She ultimately becomes obtainable, and his hands freeze as
he tries to touch her one last time;
A fatal love that has engulfed him, was her motive all along
She will finally disappear and charm another soul.

Metanoia

I walked on a path of pebbles and dust once,
abandoned and crooked all the way.
Dead leaves crunched against my cold feet,
A barren land that seldom breathes.
I wonder if someone had walked there before,
to create a new path, a route not seen before.
Helplessly revisit it several times,
hoping that my piercing yet hesitant footsteps create
a way for the water from the river to flow;
Maybe from a distance, others would find their way too. If
water found its way here,
You, nor I, would be alone again.

Come again to realize that I've always been nothing
but alone,
the process of finding a way, to create a path for me to walk
and crawl on.
That path was not born perfect,
several bumps made me trip over foolishly.
I help myself, with my head down.
Whether I crawl, walk or run,
Whether the sunshine's absence brings out my
shadow's transparency,
It will hurt all the same.

If the weeping clouds visit me again,
And my shadow disappears, leaving me unaccompanied.
Would I have reached an end?
But another cement road appeared instead.
The ending is never near, because a beginning
just happened to occur then.

Despite which direction I go, I don't look down upon
someone else's path,
Whether it be filled with woods or diamonds,
Each path was once barren like mine.

The path I walk on cannot define me.
Till I beautify it, please don't hastily judge me.
One day that's so far away,
I hope cherry blossoms will fill my feet,
Or maybe the snow will sink my feet.
If the wind sings again and hums near me, maybe it'll be a
signal that I'm not far away.

Tasnim Shahid *is a poet, writer, and author of the poetry collection titled 'With Meraki.' Her poetry encompasses the various heartfelt emotions and unspoken truths of a young adult living nothing but an ordinary life. Through these hopeless words of hers, she wishes to resonate with her readers and perhaps even spark a little hope to show them that they are not alone in their vulnerabilities and miseries.*

Poetry by

Bushra Mohamed

Cupid's Resort

In the open palms of his hands,
the ocean sways - like a woman's hips -
clear green waters, waving at me from afar.

I stare down, standing
at the edge of his fingertips,

then

I'm falling into the darkness.

but when I look up,
suspended mid-air,
I find the sea, the waves, the sand,
reflecting in his eyes,

and there she is, love, sitting on a swing,
laughing

Crush

what is a heart?
I don't think I know.
It seems to stop
when you're near me
and when I feel you close to me
I am close to God.

but God must've left me defective
because oxygen is now your breath
and I'd rather not breathe
without you.

A Bow

it was a beautiful morning
before it was ever an unforgettable night
days, of music, drink, and dancing
nights, quiet, my head on your shoulder
your voice reminds me of the breeze
and yours, raises gooseflesh on my arms
we have a summer house
we built it in our dreams
we have a winter cabin
and a fireplace, lit by our warm bodies
waves upon waves
eons of searching
my soul
and my soul

hit by a poisoned tip of an arrow.

A Black Sea

you always said,
"my dreams are violent,
my dreams are dreams of you"
bloodless sunsets and stones
chucked at my face.

but I breathed life into you
didn't I?

and wished I were dead instead.

and humanity was unfound
deprived of reciprocated touch
and pixelated endearments

in the little place we call home,
love of my love
I discard my clothes by the sea

where the air bears no scent of
your skin
and finally,

I can breathe.

Toxicity On The Dinner Table

do damnable thoughts make a damned individual;
I want to die
a relentless wheel, the driving brain, finding comfort only,
in sleep.

with a ravenous resentment,
dog-like, of an unbroken wrist,
and does it show?
the guilt foaming around my mouth,
for my foolish manipulations and knowing maneuverings
an infantile behavior for the inner possessive
seething with unadulterated jealousy;
lacking and craving, needing and wanting,
all the good things - a kiss, a touch, a romantic gesture -
all the filth - the shouting, the fragile ego, the broken
plates-

but no, I look at another and ask them:
die with me.

Bushra Mohamed *finds solace in reading and writing poetry, and has become extraordinarily passionate in receiving and sharing poems. Bushra majored in political science, works in the morning, writes at night, and is rightfully outspoken and fierce.*

Poetry by

Maryam Al Shawab

The Union Of Water And Fire

Water was promised to Fire
and got married on a Friday
with doubt pulsing through
her temple

But she loved Fire

Water was a transparent woman
and Fire barely spoke, his thoughts
conveyed through frowns and grunts

But she loved Fire

Water was the type to go with the
flow, patiently, making peace with
Fire's rage and hot-headed nature

Because she loved Fire

Water spent her life asking Fire to calm
down. Fire spent his life breaking clocks,
mugs, dishes, and her butterfly-shaped jar

But she loved Fire

Water spent her time outside, away
from Fire, to garden and grow tomatoes,
strawberries and watermelons

But she loved Fire

Water reminded herself of the way Fire's
arms, wrapped around her, made her
feel warm and safe

Because she loved Fire

Water argued with Fire for making
the cashier cry at the grocery store,
her hope for change vanishing

But she loved Fire

Water yelled at Fire more frequently
till she cursed the day she married him
she cried and cried and cried

She no longer loved Fire

Duality

Hell and heaven are lovers
their people clash at their
bellies when they embrace

Black Marker

The romance novel struck
fear into the heart of her
mother

It might as well had been
the devil laying on her
daughter's lap

Whispering corrupting thoughts
that her mother must shield
from her daughter's mind

She ran a black marker along
the words, erasing words like
hands holding, blushing, heart
fluttering, longing, arms wrapping
around, laughing

No joy, no sweetheart, no honey
could escape her ink until the
whole book was a giant blot
unreadable

She is too afraid of her daughter
craving a kind of love that involved
the soft touch of a lover's hands
only to end up her whole life starving
or fooled

"Love is a bad thing," her mother says,
her eyes filled with urgency, "Romance

is bad, it doesn't exist, it only exists
in the imagination of the Westerners
like Santa and the tooth fairy."

Her daughter doesn't know them yet,
men, and how they don't know how to
love, only disappoint, they are happy takers
and whiny givers

And yet nothing would make her mother
happier than the day she would see
her daughter marry one of them

In Love

I read a book
and thought in words

I watched a movie
and thought in scenes

I looked at a painting
and thought in colors

I played the piano
and thought in tunes

I licked ice cream
and thought in flavors

I stared at people
and thought in pictures

I counted the flowers
and thought in numbers

I looked into your eyes
and thought in love

Maryam Al Shawab *is a writer who studied media. She loves spending her time studying languages, making up stories, and admiring the moon.*

Poetry by

Maryam A. Wajdi

December 3

I sat under the window,
My knees pressed to my chest

It was right before midday,
And the sun peeked
Through the slight opening
And I thought, if only you could see
The world the way I did.

I looked at my feet, adorned with
My anklet that carried
The good summer days,
Where strangers came and then
As friends
They departed.

I looked through the opening
And the ray of light whitened my vision,
But my left eye glimpsed my reflection
Off the white ceramic tiled wall.

I remembered the days,
Sitting at the same place,
But fall had painted the morning sky
A swallowing grey.
And tears had fallen down my reddened face.

I face the sun,
And draw in its tender warmth.

I close my eyes and see your broken smiles,
Your broken heart;

We stayed on the same boat,
Parted by the same bark;
It moved farther away from the shore.

You were watching the shallow waters.

Helianthus II

You've come to me
On a summer
Day.

A swift; cool breeze
A visitor,
To the warm; invigorating air.

Yet you were yellow
Cutting through
The enduring blue.

The warmest force
Like
The glistening dew;
The fiery fullness

Inside of me.

You were like a flower

Your petals delicate.
Your complexion radiant

In the indefinite shade of the scorching sun.

You were alone,
Rooted in sorrow.

Yet

The humble
Faced the sun.

My beloved;
The Sunflower.

Man Of The Ethereal Being

Every day is the same,
I take what lies in front of me

I drag the weight on my slender feet
But it is when I fall
Into his selflessness,
That I find myself afloat.

His gentle air drifts,
Unwavering,
Cups my being as I drop
Through the soft blue sky
And cotton white cushions.

The breeze holds me
Like angels' steady lifting
And he is the heaven
All believers are seeking.

With his hands he carries hope,
His fingertips caress me.
His breath by my ear,
The sound of waves
Crashing on the shore.

The sea calls his name,
Drawing depth to the surface;
His compassion beaches
On the soft ivory's everlasting.

How can a man be so good
That he and nature appear
As one?

He is nowhere near
A person,
His love is for the world.

The Weight Of You

I sat on the edge of my bed
and felt the pang of your betrayal.

I traveled back to our adolescent days,
where you were the winter gust
to my rustling leaves and
the summer breeze to my evening sea.

We were two opposites,
yet halves apart in bodies.
I smiled at your smiles
and wept to your cries.

You were a habit,
every day and every night.

We would spend nights together
and as we faced each other,
tucked in bed,
you would tell me everything

and it would be like
I shared your burdens all along.

Or perhaps carried them all.

At that point in time,
I became familiar-
under your load I called home.

As I begin to drift away,
like the last wind on
the last winter day,

I find myself longing
for those days.

To Ruins

Years have passed
And I am still weak.
My knees trembling;
My lips, a quivering slant.

Every day, my breath grows
Weak.
Every day, weaker than
The day before.

Morning, the sun comes up.
My eyes are wide,
Terror stricken.
My sight blinded by
Dark lightness.

That throughout the day,
I am lost in clear space.
I am lost in simple words,
Safe, almost a labyrinth.

Time has left the past;
Time is racing towards
The end,
Perhaps towards death.

Even now, in your love
I am drowning
An illusion,
Alone.

I've left you
Along the seconds
One- several years ago.

I've left you,
Yet I've been drowning
With you,
Alone.

I've forsaken love as foolish.

I've abandoned what might
Have been pure and sheer happiness.

Yet at the pulse of your very existence,
At the singing sound of your name,

I die a thousand deaths.

At the touch of your hands-
No- in your love,
I perish.

Maryam A. Wajdi *is a young Emirati poet and writer, with a bachelor's degree in business management and a minor in English literature from the American University in Dubai. She specializes in poetry; her work "My Dear" and "Kiss" were previously published in Cinnamon Press's poetry magazine, Envoi.*

Poetry by

Shahd Thani

You Can't Have It All
Inspired by Barbara Ras

But you can have the moments before the *Fajr Athaan*
begins,
when your tongue swells with hopes and prayers.
You shake slumber as the mosques rise in a crescendo
with the call to prayer and bulbuls sing praising Allah.
You can cup your hands to hold the overflowing prayers;
to embrace your loved ones- the departed, and for the
coming days.

You can have the rose gold light as the sun rises
stretching lazy fingers to caress you as you journal in bed
while you sink your soul deeper into paragraphs and
pillows.
You can have cats lounging on welcome mats,
yawning as you brush past them.

You can have the first cup of flat white
at your favorite café and the first smiles.
You can have the wonder your father carries
as he wanders through alleyways in the streets of old Dubai
You can have your mother waiting for you to come home,
because she always worries when you are late.
You can have the banter of siblings watching a movie

You can have conversations with your godsons,
where you have answers to all their questions
and worry about the day when you no longer
have the answers or are no longer "cool" to a child.
You can have their hugs when they squeeze you

with all their might and you hold on.
You just hold on to that tiny but fierce love.

You may not always have the Saturday breakfast dates
or the Tuesday coffee dates but you will always have
those connections that fill you up and bring out the best in
you.

You can have the dream of Japan, the little cottage in Kyoto,
and riding trains throughout the seasons to fill you with
wonder.
You can have your notebook to build worlds,
and friends that feel so real to you

You can have empathy as you watch the world around you
and the intuition to know that you might not have it all.
But what you have is rich like *dibs* dripping over *Chebab*.
This is love and it is all that matters.

Wife
After Ada Limon

"*Inshallah* we celebrate you as a bride in white."
"We want to wear ballgowns and dance at your wedding."
"We hope to see your arms decorated with henna."
"*Inshallah* we see you holding your son."
Did you say *Ameen*? Say *Ameen*.
All around me, hands held up in prayer
for everyone's joy but mine.

This imaginary wedding, this imaginary husband,
always chasing after me like a looming ghost,
a dark presence but most of all a threat.
Am I not enough? Am I not whole?

I wonder what happens after festivities
when brides let their plastered smiles rest,
turn to the stranger next to them who became theirs
and those voices oh-so-knowing telling her
what is deemed "wife-like, wife-worthy"
until she forgets the sound of her own voice.

Wife, this heavy word that sounds like strife
but everyone tells me is another step into life.
Duty that turns your life upside down.
But can you ever ask for the same? It's not done.
It's *Aib*. A man is a man, after all. You can't change them.

Husband, this stranger people often tell me
I would have to raise like my child, feed him,
clothe him and make sure he never wants for anything.
Always waiting for him to come back from a life unchanged.

A wife is someone obligated into roles inherited from
mothers and foremothers.
She is wife of the man, mother of the son, *Umm* her
firstborn –
– until she forgets even her own name.

A wife is demure, serves *gahwa* to elders, and smiles
prettily,
even when she's crying on the inside.
Always juggling. Never enough.

All these thoughts run through my mind at every wedding.
And then a matron squeezes my hand with tears in her eyes
to reassure me that I'm next *"Uqbalech, habibity uqbalech"*

What's the word for someone who hears the clash of cages
instead of wedding bells? She who tears a hole in the earth
with the grief
of lives unlived. She who holds a universe within her and
doesn't want
to be diminished. She who is whole with or without a man
in life,
But deep-down wonders at the soulmate who
complements instead of erases,
the partner to navigate rocky oceans with, and dream of a
life led in purpose together.

Rise

You lie awake at night
rocking in a sea of treacherous thoughts.
Your baby cries with wants
you no longer understand,
burrowing against your aching heart.
He sleeps on your side of the bed
afraid of his father's shadow.
You wonder if you sacrificed
too much, too soon.

You used to think happily ever after
meant doing it all.
You could be whatever you chose to be:
The woman, the wife, the mother
the writer, the painter, the philosopher.

You thought you could dream the dreams
that soar into dizzying heights
You forgot the miracles
that only you can perform.
The magic that only you can weave

Bringing a child into the world
was an earthquake, except you were
the only one who shook.
You tremble with the ripple
of rightness and responsibility
holding your child,
your tangible hope,
your comfort,
your blessing against you.

You thought you could be
whatever you chose to be
Nobody told you that you
would give up your own femininity or
that you would forget the glory of your talents.

Nobody told you that you would
have to be the mother and father
Because Daddy is too busy
playing PlayStation with his friends.

Because the only time Daddy carries your baby
is to pose with him for a picture on Instagram
So everyone can see what a perfect father he is.

When you are the one who should see.
You are the witness to his life, to this life,
and in your eyes, you have the power
to make loved ones grow.

Rise,
rise and rise again
until you learn the breadth of your own music.

Rise as you learn to love yourself
as deeply as you want to be loved.
Learn to be selfish sometimes,
to be brave.
Learn to cry sometimes.

Rise and Rise again.

You are your own phoenix.
Learn to become and un-become.
Learn to dance over your own ashes like a ballerina.
Learn to smile
Learn to laugh

Let the ice thaw off your bruised heart
Ignite and know the fiery heat of your burning passions
Ignite for you can burn down a city with your own fire
Rise and know that in burning aflame, there is healing
Know that in breaking, you can only be fixed
Rise and rise again
into and unto yourself.

Sink into the solace of your own being
Never for him.
It was never about him.
Rise and rise again.
Tower with the strength of your roaring heart.
This is your story.
You are the poet.
Hold the pen
with courage.
Don't let your hand tremble.
Tell your story fearlessly
You are the master of your own destiny
You have the magic wand
You can spin miracles
Finally, sing and rejoice
For you have always, always
Been beautiful.

Cosmopolitan Man

He walks in labels like a peacock
The cosmopolitan man from UAE
With his stiff *Kandoora* rustling
as he hurries, picking up his step
to show off his Gucci sandals
and the fact that he matched it
with his brand-new cap.

He readjusts it just so you notice
Trying not to smirk from behind
his Ray-Ban aviators.

On his iPhone glimpses of Snapchat
It rings and he speaks into the Airpod.
Hooded gaze glancing at you ever-so-casually
I'm wanted. I'm special. But there's room for you too.

He walks proudly, shoulders back
chest puffed up with his own importance
strutting like a Kanye before he found his Kim.
It could be you.
He takes off his cap and runs a hand through his perfectly coiffed
hair and gives a long-suffering sigh.

You don't know what you're missing, he seems to say
And though his beauty does make a girl's heart pound
Long black lashes and a perfectly trimmed beard
A salute to the modern Bedouin, but a reminder that
he could have walked off a Lois Vuitton ad
with lips that know all the lines to reel a woman in.

There he goes with his soulful eyes
Oh, and here comes the pang of longing
and the heavy knowledge that for all his beauty
He is just a shell of all that he could be.

There are no longer heroes for the modern woman
Chivalry is dead along with the dream of the knight
On a white charger to rescue you from the dragons of this
age

Where is the hero?
Where is the poet?
The Scholar?
The wizard?
And just who is this poor cosmopolitan
woman supposed to hold out for?

Shahd Thani *is an Emirati romance writer, poet, and the winner of the first Emirates Literature Foundation Mentorship award. Her poetry revolves around the frustrations of being a woman, adulthood, and romance. She mentors younger writers, hosts writing workshops and book clubs, and enjoys celebrating the written word.*